WORLDLY ESCAPES

Across America and Around the Globe

Writers: **Victoria Patience and Rob Tallia**

Editorial Director: **Laura M. Kidder**

Design Director: **Joerg Metzner**

Art Director: **Jodie Knight**

Photo Editor: **Cherie Cincilla**

Design Production: **Joe Rockey, Jenii Stewart**

Product Management Director: **Jenny Thornton**

Production: **Carey Seren**

Published in U.S.A.
Printed in China

For licensing information and copyright
permissions, contact us at
permissions@randmcnally.com

If you have a comment, suggestion,
or even a compliment,
please visit us at
randmcnally.com/contact
or write to
Rand McNally Consumer Affairs
P.O. Box 7600
Chicago, Illinois 60680-9915

1 2 3 LE 18 17 16

Front cover: Florence, Italy: Basilica di Santa Maria del Fiore (Basilica of
Saint Mary of the Flower). **Back cover:** Around Sedona, AZ: formation views
near Schnebly Hill Road.

Contents

Urban Immersions

Cultural Pursuits

Contents
(Continued)

A Sense of the World

Fully experiencing the world means not only taking in its sights but also its aromas, sounds, flavors, *and* textures. And the escapes in this book are designed to awaken all your senses.

Let your eyes blaze amid Utah's red rocks or Namibia's orange dunes; let them cool amid turquoise South Pacific seas or deep-blue Pacific Northwest bays. Be surrounded by rainbows of color in Holland's tulip fields, Arizona's Painted Desert, and Australia's Great Barrier Reef. Be dazzled by opulence in Newport's Gilded Age estates, St. Petersburg's tsarist palaces, and the Loire Valley's regal châteaux.

Wake up and smell the estate-grown coffee at a Colombian plantation. Note the hint of lavender on the salty breeze in the Dungeness River Valley and the strong scent of sulfur at geothermal wonders in Iceland and Hawaii and Wyoming. Breathe in a complex medley of aromas in Zanzibar's spice markets.

Strain your ears to untangle the chorus of wildlife at a Costa Rican eco-lodge; merrily join in the chorus of a traditional ballad in an Irish pub. Embrace the pounding of carnival drums in Brazil and of your heart on the steep slopes of the Rockies—both American and Canadian. Let the roaring wall of water that is Africa's Victoria Falls drown out the sound of everything else.

Try to tease apart the ingredients of a Mexican *mole* or an Indian curry. Note how falling cherry blossoms caress your cheek with equal tenderness amid the stately grandeur of Washington monuments and the spiritual tranquility of Kyoto temple gardens. Ease tensions you didn't know you had during powerful Thai massages or warming soaks in Colorado mineral springs.

And then there's your sixth sense: the thrill as you spot a lion in Kenya, a Komodo dragon in Indonesia, or an alligator in the Everglades. The shiver as you survey the remains of great civilizations in Cambodia, Peru, and the American Southwest.

Can you sense that it's time to escape into the world?

Tulip fields, The Netherlands

Urban Immersions

"I have an affection for a great city. I feel safe in the neighborhood of man, and enjoy the sweet security of the streets."

—*Henry Wadsworth Longfellow*

Barcelona: Detail of Antoni Gaudí's Casa Batlló.

An Imperial Treasure

Russia's tsars knew all about bling. Nowhere is this more evident than the baroque riot of gilt and marble that is the Winter Palace. Indeed, the entire Hermitage complex on the river Neva in central St. Petersburg is as artful as the imperial jewelry, furnishings, and works by Rembrandt and other masters within. A short walk east along the river Moyka brings you to the mosaic-covered, onion-domed Church of the Savior on Spilled Blood, built on the assassination site of Alexander II. He and other tsars now rest in the cathedral at the Peter and Paul Fortress, an island stronghold near the Neva's north bank. Climb the bell tower to behold the city that was once the heart of their empire.

St. Petersburg: Winter Palace interior;
Church of the Savior on Spilled Blood (right).

Buildings along the water in Copenhagen's Nyhavn district.

Designs on Scandinavia

One look at the smooth arms and curving back, and you're smitten . . . with Hans Wegner's Round Chair. You fall for other Danish beauties at the Designmuseum and stores like Illums Bolighus, where textiles and ceramics are packable objects of your affection. Other great Danes along the pedestrian-only Strøget include Royal Copenhagen (for china) and Georg Jensen (for silver). At a canal-side café, amid Nyhavn's 17th-century townhouses, people-watching leads to guessing which local designers are behind the simple but stylish looks that Københavners do so well. Wood Wood? Mads Nørgaard? Samsøe & Samsøe? Food here is also artfully designed—from the organic hotdogs at DØP, a stand near the Round Tower, to the 20-course education in new Nordic cuisine that is dinner at Noma.

Underground Art

The air is damp and chalky, the light dim. But you're reluctant to resurface. The Berliner Unterwelten tour's abandoned U-bahn stations and escape tunnels are fascinating. So is the contemporary art at the Sammlung Boros gallery, in a topside WW II air-raid bunker, and at the Hamburger Bahnhof. On Museum Island, amid the river Spree, the artifacts were excavated long ago, and the art is more classical. At the open-air East Side Gallery, the art is painted straight on the wall—what's left of the Berlin Wall, that is—though today's hottest graffiti is in the countercultural Kreuzberg district. At night, re-submerge into a Berlin supper club and then swim in a sea of crowds and Techno at nightspots like Tresor or Berghain Panorama Bar.

Berlin: Alte Nationalgalerie on Museum Island; Berlin Wall (right).

A Tale of One City

London is the main character in many a Charles Dickens novel. The hard times he documented are gone, but not glimpses of the city he venerated. Follow in David Copperfield's footsteps over London Bridge and past St Paul's Cathedral. Stop for victuals at Fleet Street's Ye Olde Cheshire Cheese, a 300-year-old pub Dickens frequented. In Bloomsbury, see the desk on which *Oliver Twist* was written at the Charles Dickens Museum. Southwest in Covent Garden, the Charles Dickens Coffee House stands (amid high-street boutiques) where his newspaper offices once did (amid vegetable shops). Across Trafalgar Square and down Whitehall is another great London symbol: Big Ben. Fulfill still more great expectations by paying respects to many British wordsmiths in Westminster Abbey's Poets' Corner.

London: Westminster Abbey's Poets' Corner (left); Big Ben and Houses of Parliament.

L'Arôme de Paris

Coco Chanel once said, "A woman who doesn't wear perfume has no future." That's not you. Dressed in your chicest travel outfit—this is Paris, after all—your future holds a fragrant day amid vials antique and new at the Fragonard Perfume Museum and Galeries Lafayettes. South of Place Vendôme, Shiseido superstar Serge Lutens provokes with contemporary scents like Tubéreuse Criminelle, and vintage bouquets fill the air at nearby Jovoy. Along the Seine, floral notes come attached to stems at the Jardins des Tuileries; west along the Champs-Elysées, they fill expensive bottles at the boutiques of Annick Goutal and Guerlain— the original *parfumier Parisien*. Stock up on more-accessible fragrances at French cosmetics superstore Sephora. Savor the sweet smell of success at the Arc de Triomphe.

Louvre Museum and Tuileries Gardens; Arc de Triomphe (right).

A Rich Mosaic

Lisbon's Golden Age edict seems to have been: Conquer the world or tile it. In the spirit of Vasco da Gama, you start exploring waterside, at the ornate Belém Tower. The riches are exhaustive in the nearby Jerónimos Monastery and National Coach Museum. Fortify yourself at Pastéis de Belém, where the custard tarts are as sublime as the walls covered in blue-and-white *azulejos* (tiles). Later, you see how such artful murals evolved from North African designs at the National Tile Museum and the Fronteira Palace. As night falls, mournful *fado* music fills cafés in Alfama, an ancient, labyrinthine district below the Moorish São Jorge Castle. You settle in for a culturally rich end to a treasure-filled day.

Lisbon: Belém Tower (left); garden at Fronteira Palace.

Barcelona Up and Down

Look up. The spindly spires and curved facades of Antoni Gaudí's Sagrada Família seem to have sprung from Barcelona's soil organically. The basilica, just one of Gaudí's urban treasures, has grown at a vegetative pace, too—since 1882 and with a completion date of 2028. Look down and around. Wander La Rambla and the Barri Gòtic district, channeling Pablo Picasso and Joan Miró. Dare to drink *cava* (Spanish sparkling wine) from a *porrón*. Savor *crema catalana* (like crème brûlée only better). Up and inland, things get surreal at Salvador Dalí museums in Púbol and Figueres and medieval in Girona's Barri Vell. Down along the coast, Tarragona and its seaside Roman ruins are Catalan classics.

Sagrada Família Basilica—inside and out.

Florence Alfresco

Vermilion. Ultramarine. Burnt umber. All so rich they might have been painted onto wet plaster only yesterday. Among Florence's stunning Renaissance frescoes are those by Masaccio and Domenico Ghirlandaio (and his apprentice, Michelangelo) in the Santa Maria Novella Basilica. Nearby, in San Lorenzo's equally vivid markets, stock up on crusty bread, wild-boar salami, creamy mozzarella, heirloom tomatoes, olives, and a bottle of Chianti. Head a few miles uphill along villa-lined lanes to Fiesole. Find a shady picnic spot near the town's San Francesco Monastery, and feast your eyes on the orange-red roofs of Florence. Dream up more colorful adventures over dinner at a Florentine restaurant, beside a piazza and under the Tuscan moon.

Basilica di Santa Maria del Fiore (Basilica of Saint Mary of the Flower, left);
piazza overlooking the river Arno and beyond.

Game of Stones

Sentinels once paced the stone ramparts above Croatia's walled city of Dubrovnik. Like you, they looked out at the Adriatic's turquoise, island-dotted waters or down on the terra-cotta roofs of the Romanesque houses. Over the centuries, so many people have walked along Stradun, the main street, that its limestone flags are polished to a shine. You follow in their footsteps to Gundulic Square—channeling *Game of Thrones,* as Old Town is the stand-in for King's Landing—and settle in to sip an Istra Bitter (think: Croatian Campari). Later, you'll catch a ferry to Hvar Island, where Europe's elite lounge in promenade bars. Tomorrow, you'll trade fashionistas for fishermen and palms for pines on quiet Mljet, with its horseshoe-shaped port and forested national park.

Watery views of Dubrovnik, Croatia.

City views and market scenes, Fez, Morocco.

A Maze of Souks

Centuries-old buildings crowd the medieval medina's lanes in Fez, once Morocco's capital. Donkeys and bicycles compete with pedestrians. In the Aïn Allou souk, sunlight filters through overhead grilles onto the embroidery of artfully arranged *babouches* (slippers). A djellaba-clad shopkeeper invites you to his roof terrace to see the old city's renowned tanneries and bargain fiercely for leather goods. Amid elaborate *zellij* tiles and carved cedar, you behold exquisite Fassi and Berber craftsmanship (minus the haggling) at the 14th-century Bou Inania madrasa and the Nejjarine Museum of Wood Arts and Crafts. Back in the souks, while shopping for metal fretwork lanterns and earthenware tajine pots, you lose your way—utterly. That's OK. To find Fez, you have to get lost in it.

A Natural Beauty

The cable car leaves the station and begins to revolve. Your stomach plunges. Your jaw drops. Table Mountain is in the heart of Cape Town, and the 3,500-foot plateau is just one of the city's natural attractions. On its eastern slopes, the Kirstenbosch National Botanical Gardens have 7,000 indigenous plant species. South of the city is one of Africa's southernmost points: the craggy Cape of Good Hope. As you hike, cycle, or drive to it, watch for baboons, zebras, and antelope. At Boulders Beach, you might see African penguins or southern right whales. To really toast nature's bounty, though, head east of Cape Town to the Stellenbosch and Franschhoek winelands for a glass of South Africa's signature Pinotage.

Cape Town: Table Mountain Aerial Cableway and Kirstenbosch National Botanical Gardens; Boulders Beach (right).

Old City, New Tricks

Bolts of sari silk, bowls of bindi powder, stacks of vegetables—the rainbow-hued wares at Colaba's crowded Lala Nigam Road market are displayed with geometrical genius. So are the finger sandwiches at the waterfront Taj Mahal Palace Hotel, where afternoon tea recalls British colonial days almost as much as the neighboring Gateway of India. You leap forward in time at the National Gallery of Modern Art, where only the facade is classical, and while touring Film City, where brightly dressed casts rehearse elaborate Bollywood-blockbuster choreographies. Some Mumbai traditions transcend time: like jostling through busy streets, perhaps to Chaupati Beach, where the drama of the 10-day Ganesh Chaturthi festival unfolds each year and where food stalls sell India's classic (and often spicy) treats year-round.

Mumbai: Taj Mahal Palace Hotel and Gateway to India;
Lord Ganesh processional and market spices (right).

China Goes Global

Shanghai's riverfront Bund district offers a living lesson on the changing face of China. The Neoclassical and Art Deco buildings along its promenade once contained European banks and trading companies, which were shuttered under Communism. Like China itself, the buildings here are again well and truly open to the outside, this time with tony hotels and restaurants as well as luxury-brand flagships—both global and local. Across the Huangpu River, Shanghai's future further unfolds in the skyscrapers of Pudong, several topped with vertigo-inducing bars and restaurants. West of the waterfront, it's all about urban renewal: The Xintiandi and Tianzifang districts are now a hipster paradise, their traditional stone *shikumen* (lane houses) transformed into cafés, galleries, and boutiques.

Shanghai: Bund District (left); Pudong skyline.

Nature Worship

A pale-pink canopy stretches out before you. It's spring in Kyoto, and the canal-side Philosopher's Walk is the perfect place for *hanami*, viewing the cherry blossoms. The path takes you past Zen shrines like Ginkaku-ji and Nanzen-ji, just two of the city's 2,000 temples. Meticulously raked sand gardens and tree-ringed ponds invite reflection—now and when the grounds are deep in snow or alight with fall color. The setting is equally beautiful and spiritual in the dense, unearthly bamboo groves at Arashiyama, a district on the city's western outskirts. Your meditations continue north of town, as you soak in the *onsen* (hot springs) at Kurama, then hike past shrines to another traditional mountain village, Kibune, where restaurant seating overlooks a rushing river.

Kyoto: Otagi Nenbutsu-ji Temple (left) and bamboo grove, Arashiyama District.

Harboring Culture

Outbound aboard the Manly Ferry, you see two of Sydney's cultural icons against the cloudless sky: the arching Harbour Bridge, which you might yet climb, and the sail-like Opera House, where you might yet see a show. Beyond the headland lie the eastern beaches: Yesterday, you brunched at Bondi before following the 4-mile trail past Tamarama to Bronte, with its surfers and other beautiful people, and Coogee, with its seawater swimming pools. As the inbound ferry approaches Circular Quay, you spot the Museum of Contemporary Art. Tomorrow, you might explore it or head beyond the skyscrapers to quieter neighborhoods like Surry Hills, where Aussie dining and designing vie for your attention. For now, the main attraction is the harbor backlit by the sunset.

Sydney: Bondi Beach; Opera House (right).

Where Africa Meets Brazil

A steady drum and accompanying *twang* of a single-stringed gourd instrument, the *berimbau,* reverberate through Salvador da Bahia's Pelourinho district. In the shadow of a baroque church, two practitioners of *capoeira*—a form of African martial arts mixed with dance and acrobatics that evolved on colonial sugar plantations—face off. Amid the Rio Vermelho district's food stalls, the soundtrack features lapping waves and sizzling vats of *dendê* (palm) oil. A smiling cook in a voluminous white skirt hands you *acarajé,* a black-eyed-pea fritter with tomatoes, shrimp, and hot sauce. Night brings the supercharged rehearsals of carnival *blocos* (street bands) like Ilê Aiyê or Olodum. In Brazil's capital of African culture, everyone moves to different beat.

Salvador da Bahia: modern harbor; colonial street scenes (right).

Lima on the Plate

The sightseeing menu in Latin America's culinary capital looks promising. You whet your appetite for Spanish Colonial history in and around Plaza Mayor, where the baroque cathedral and exquisite Casa de Aliaga are delectable architectural amuse-bouches. Next up? An appetizer of pre-Columbian culture—amid textiles and ceramics at the Larco Museum or amid ruins at the Huaca Pucllana temple complex in Miraflores. This district's restaurants put Peru on the gastronomic map. So, for the main course (literally this time), you sample ceviche and other seafood at La Mar or modern takes on classic Andean fare at Central. For dessert, succumb to an artisanal chocolate confection. Watching the sun set over the Pacific on a walk along El Malecón makes a nice finish.

Huaca Pucllana temple complex (left); cathedral and Plaza Mayor.

Everything, All at Once, Together

Cirque du Soleil acrobats wow. Seinfeld kills. David Copperfield disappears. The High Roller, the world's tallest observation wheel lifts you above it all at 550 feet. And we do mean *all*. The 4-mile extravaganza that is the Las Vegas Strip has more than just neon-lit casinos. It's a blitzkrieg of entertainments, from endless buffets and five-star restaurants to lounge acts and magic shows to slanted elevators and a replica Eiffel Tower. You've posed with a Roman centurion at Caesars Palace, uncovered vintage Vegas in the sign boneyard at the Neon Museum, eaten like royalty at Aureole in Mandalay Bay, and danced all night at XS Las Vegas in the Wynn. What's next? The choreographed fountain spectacle at the Bellagio. Egyptian splendor at the Luxor. A thrill ride *atop* the 1,149-foot Stratosphere . . . .

Las Vegas: Neon Museum;
High Roller observation wheel (right).

On the Beach

Is life any finer than where the City of Angels meets the deep-blue Pacific? Not when you can rent a cozy Venice Beach bungalow and take an early morning stroll or jog along the boardwalk, greeting some of the neighborhood's finest (and weirdest) locals in the process. As the sun rises still higher, bike along the beach to Santa Monica for a tapas lunch at Blue Stove and some shopping on the Third Street Promenade. Hit the pier for a sunset Ferris wheel ride, and return to Venice for dinner at Gjelina on hip Abbot Kinney Boulevard. End the evening with a cold brew from one of oceanfront Venice Ale House's 32 taps. That's a wrap, folks!

Santa Monica Pier, Los Angeles

Pike Place Market, Seattle

Flying Fish

From the first cup at Starbucks' oldest operating store (circa 1976) to the last call at Pike Brewing Company, Seattle's iconic market bustles. Pike Place is truly a microcosm of everything that's cool about the Emerald City: salmon-tossing fishmongers, artisanal cheese makers, local artists, acrobatic buskers, a gum wall, a 500-pound bronze piggy bank. There's enough wholesome, quirky, Pacific Northwest fun to fill a day and a night. If you need a quiet break, stroll to the nearby Olympic Sculpture Park for oversized art amid sizable water views. Later, sample the city's acclaimed cuisine, perhaps back at Matt's in the Market, where you have Pike Place purveyors to thank for your fresh feast.

A Blues Wind Blowin'

Winter. The wind whips through snow-covered streets as the last of the day's commuters straggle home. You? You're cozy in a blues club, somewhere (well, *anywhere*) in Chicago. Perhaps you're in the Loop, the very heart of it all, grooving to one of Buddy Guy's Legends—or even the master himself. Or maybe you're boogying down up north in Lincoln Park at B.L.U.E.S. or the classic Kingston Mines. Or why not in Logan Square at Rosa's Lounge or at Blue Chicago in River North? The options are as endless as the city's thirst for blues music . . . just ask the half-million fans that come for summer's massive Chicago Blues Festival.

Frozen Chicago River (left); a Windy City blues club.

The Heart of French Canada

You finish your croissant and café au lait, pay the check with a *"merci beaucoup,"* and head out to window-shop on cobbled rue du Petit Champlain. It feels like France—there's even a turreted chateau and a fort to keep out the British—but on the funicular ride to Haute-Ville, the St. Lawrence River views wash away the illusion. Québec's capital is staunchly French, but the nearby Laurentian Mountains and 275-foot Montmorency Falls are decidedly Canadian. So are the winters. Do as the locals do: Embrace the season during the two-week carnival or by tobogganing or skating in Plains of Abraham park. Warm up with a Caribou: hot red wine and rum sweetened with, *bien sûr,* maple syrup.

Québec City: Rue Ste-Ursule; Fairmont Le Château Frontenac hotel
towering above the old city (right).

A Necklace of Emeralds

An angler dips a line into Jamaica Pond, hoping to catch some trout or salmon, while herons and egrets fish for their own dinner in the Back Bay Fens. Miles away, in America's oldest city park—Boston Common—a Shakespeare troupe sets up for its annual offering of The Bard. Early in the morning, golfers tee off in Franklin Park while gardeners water the exquisite offerings at the Arnold Arboretum. Planned by Frederick Law Olmstead in the 1800s, the so-called Emerald Necklace circles Boston, uniting its green spaces and linking all the action. But the city didn't rest on its laurels—its 20-year-long Big Dig project buried enough traffic to create a topside sculpture-filled network of new parks that is the Rose Fitzgerald Kennedy Greenway.

Boston: Pond at Public Garden (left); Boston Common.

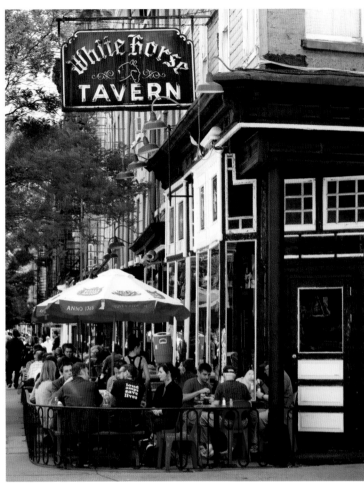

All Around the Village

Stand in New York City's Washington Square Park, perhaps under the Washington Arch. Close your eyes. Make a wish. Whatever you desire is probably less than a mile away. First, you might play a game of chess, grab a hot dog from a cart, and watch the buskers strut. Then you head west, perhaps, for jazz at the Village Vanguard, a pint at the White Horse Tavern, or cupcakes at Magnolia Bakery. Or maybe you'll head east for some skull-shaped confections at Bond Street Chocolate and some poetry at KGB Bar. For a memorable dinner at Gotham and vintage shopping at Beacon's Closet, venture north. For brick-oven pizza at Arturo's and indie rock at Mercury Lounge, travel south. This is the Village—alive in all directions.

New York City: Washington Square Park; White Horse Tavern (right).

Framing Freedom

The room is quiet, the chairs empty. Still, it's not hard to imagine what happened here in July of 1776: Benjamin Franklin, Thomas Jefferson, John Adams, John Hancock, and dozens of others, debating the final wording of the document that signaled this nation's secession from England. You're standing in Independence Hall, where both the Declaration of Independence and the United States Constitution were signed, and just steps from the Liberty Bell and other key colonial sites in Philadelphia's Old City. Take your time visiting the Betsy Ross House, birthplace of the American flag; strolling the cobblestones of Elfreth's Alley, America's oldest continuously inhabited street; and paying homage to Franklin and other framers of American freedom at the Christ Church Burial Ground.

Philadelphia: Independence Hall and
the Liberty Bell; Elfreth's Alley (right).

Capital Grandeur

Day and night, D.C. is a commanding study of shadow and light. The Washington Monument rises 555 feet above the National Mall, its white-marble image doubled in the sun-drenched reflecting pool. From the top, vistas stretch to the capitol dome, the city, and out to Virginia and Maryland. You also see the neoclassical columns of your next destination: the Lincoln Memorial. The great man's likeness sits amid insight-etched walls: ". . . *that we here highly resolve that these dead shall not have died in vain . . .*" Contemplate his words under the famous cherry trees, whose stands blossom into springtime bouquets. Darkness falls; the spotlights shine. Ahead is the grandeur of the domed Jefferson Memorial, sublimely reflected in the Tidal Basin.

Lincoln Memorial facing the Washington Monument (left);
Jefferson Memorial

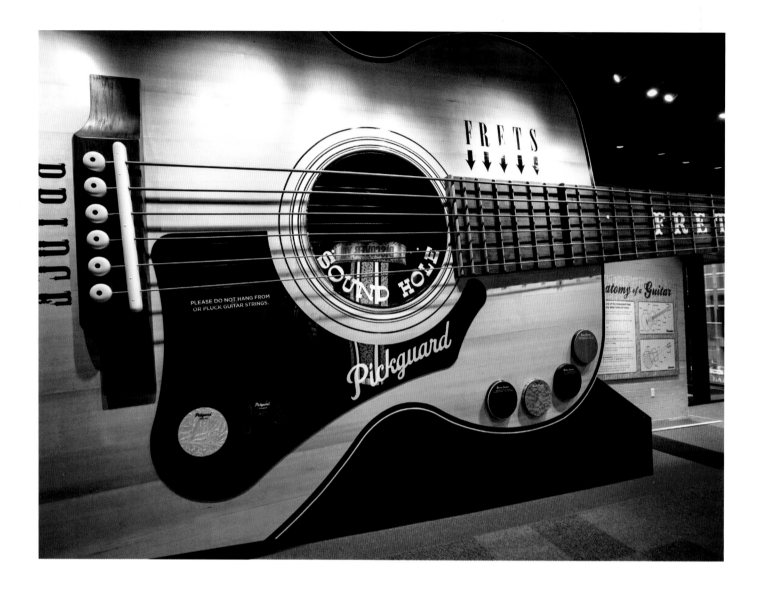

A Night at the Opry

It's just after midnight. Most of America is asleep, but in Nashville, Sarah Gayle Meech takes the stage at Robert's Western World. Time for another toe-tappin' set of live honky-tonk . . . the heck with tomorrow. Here, in the epicenter of country music, no matter what you're doing or where you are—coffee shop, bar, taxicab—the sweet sounds of Patsy Cline and Loretta Lynn will follow you. Both women found fame at the Grand Ole Opry, home to one of America's longest-running weekly radio broadcasts and still a place to catch new talent and classic performers. Brush up on musical legends and lore with a backstage tour or a visit to the Country Music Hall of Fame and Museum and the Johnny Cash Museum.

Nashville: Country Music Hall of Fame; Broadway nightlife (right).

BIG TIME
BOOTS
THE
STAGE
ON BROADWAY
BAR-B-QUE
HONKY TONK
GRILL
ATM
Ryman
Auditorium

A Garden in the City

The Southern magnolias bloom. The crepe myrtles blossom. The live oaks billow. Wrought iron is shaped into angels and cornstalks; Victorian gingerbread adorns small shotgun houses and grand mansions alike. The St. Charles Streetcar clangs and chuffs along the northern edge of the aptly named Garden District, filled with natural and man-made New Orleans–style beauty. Solitude beckons amid the ornate tombs of Lafayette Cemetery. Camaraderie calls out from Magazine Street bars and restaurants. Book a room at the Sully Mansion Bed & Breakfast. Wander the streets, shop for curios, enjoy a Creole feast at Commander's Palace. After all, why just tour a garden when you can *live* it?

The Garden District, New Orleans

The Night Becomes You

It's twilight in Miami. Back from the beach, in your all-white room at the Philippe Starck–designed Delano Hotel, you're swapping Versace swimwear for some John Varvatos or Michael Kors. Go ahead and name-drop . . . that's what South Beach is all about. Why not revel in it over dinner at trendy Prime 112, on Art Deco–laden Ocean Drive, or beside the velvet rope outside the Fontainebleau hotel's hip LIV nightclub? For a mellower (but no less stylish) scene, stroll the buzzy Lincoln Road pedestrian mall and catch some jazz at nearby Cabaret South Beach. Even the parking garages here are chic—11 11 Lincoln Road, designed by "starchitects" Herzog & de Meuron, is the essence of postmodern cool.

Art Deco buildings along Miami's Ocean Drive.

Time Travel in Havana

It's the 1930s. Ernest Hemingway knocks back frozen daiquiris at Floridita, the bar that invented them. It's the 1940s and '50s. Brylcreemed Habaneros drive Caddies along the ocean-sprayed Malecón. Fidel Castro and Ernesto "Che" Guevara sail the *Granma* from Mexico to eastern Cuba and revolutionize the country en route to Havana. It's the 1960s. Crowds pack the vast Plaza de la Revolución for an impassioned Castro speech. It's the present. The Museo de la Revolución now occupies the Palacio Presidencial, and hip cafés now fill Old Havana's balconied, neoclassical townhouses. And yet, amid this city's vintage cars and monuments to the revolution, it's hard to tell where you are in time.

Classic balconies and a vintage Buick convertible;
Paseo de Martí (right).

Cultural Pursuits

"A nation's culture resides in the hearts and
in the soul of its people."
—*Mahatma Gandhi*

Taos Pueblo, NM

Fáilte go Gaillimh!

Welcome to Galway! In one of Ireland's *Gaeltachts,* you might just be greeted in Irish, perhaps at Tig Cóilí, a pub where the pints are pulled perfectly and the traditional music is live. You'll definitely experience Irish flavors at Sheridans Cheesemongers and Wine Bar—try the Diliskus, flecked with Atlantic seaweed. For classic Éire views, walk the Prom to the suburb of Salthill on Galway Bay. Or drive the Wild Atlantic Way south to the limestone Cliffs of Moher, rising 650 feet above roiling waters. For Aran Islands vistas, follow the trail towards Hag's Head. Then reverse the perspective on the ferry from Doolin to Inis Oírr, the smallest island, where pony traps carry you along winding lanes amid fields crisscrossed with stone walls.

County Galway, Ireland: Cliffs of Moher (left); Dún Aonghasa fort on Inis Mór, Aran Islands.

A Wee Walk

You scramble up Earl's Seat, the highest of the Campsie Fells, your hands cold but your heart warm. Is it the whisky from nearby Glengoyne Distillery or the rugged hilly view? There's much to fire your spirit while hiking or biking the well-marked trails and towpaths of Scotland's 134-mile John Muir Way. From the Firth of Clyde to the Firth of Forth, its 10 segments link feats of nature and man: Loch Lomond, the Trossachs, the Antonine Wall, Blackness Castle, Edinburgh proper, Aberlady Bay. Stop at an inn for fish and chips or haggis (if you dare); sample milder malts on lowland detours to Auchentoshan in the west or Glenkinchie in the east. Your wee walk has surely earned you a dram or two.

Scotland: Blackness Castle (top); Campsie Fells (left).

England on Location

While approaching turreted Highclere Castle, déjà vu takes hold. Upon entering, Edwardian England has you in its thrall. This Hampshire manor was the main location for television's *Downton Abbey.* Though fascinating, the tour of sumptuous reception rooms and oak-paneled stairs takes a toll. Resisting the urge to ring for Carson, you repair to a bench on the grounds. Downton's village, a stone's throw away on screen, is actually in Bampton, 40 miles north. In Oxford, 20 miles east of Bampton, centuries-old university buildings recall Harry Potter movies and *Brideshead Revisited.* You head to a pub hotel in the Cotswolds, attempting a return to reality. But you soon see why the film industry has made this region's rolling countryside synonymous with England.

Highclere Castle—the stand-in for Downton Abbey;
Cotswolds landscape (right).

Blooms by Bike

You ease off the bike pedals and slow to a halt. Over a hedge, yellow, orange, fuchsia, scarlet, and indigo flowers reach skyward. You gather speed again. The fields become a colorful quilt blanketing the earth well into the horizon. In Holland's *Bollenstreek* (bulb district), millions of tulips bloom in spring—preceded by daffodils and hyacinths and followed by gladioli and lilies. Behind you is the medieval city of Leiden, birthplace of Rembrandt. Ahead is Lisse's 79-acre Keukenhof (aka the Garden of Europe). Your 20-mile ride will end in the cobbled streets of Haarlem, once a tulip trading center. For now, the journey is the destination: There's only the wind in your hair and a sea of nodding blossoms.

Tulip fields, The Netherlands

France: Renaissance kitchen garden at Villandry (left);
Château Chenonceau and the Cher River.

A Rich Tapestry

In southern Sicily, cultural relics are woven into the terrain. The Greeks, Romans, Byzantines, Saracens, Normans, and Spanish all wanted this Mediterranean island for their own. Though most of the Doric temples near Agrigento are dramatic piles of cylindrical stone, the Temple of Concord's many columns stand tall amid knotted, centuries-old olive trees. Farther east, mosaics covering the walls and floors of Villa Romana del Casale offer surprising glimpses of Roman life: here, girls in bikinis, there, a boy on skis. To the southeast, Modica, Noto, and Ragusa show off baroque architecture; seaside Syracuse showcases Greco-Roman temples and amphitheaters. You might find it hard to leave this spectacular scenic and cultural tapestry behind—just like generations of visitors before you.

Sicily, Italy: Temple of Concord, Agrigento (left); coastline of Syracuse.

Spice Islands

The pale, thick bark's rich scent is unmistakable: It's cinnamon, ripped straight from the tree. Clove, cardamom, nutmeg, saffron, turmeric, and vanilla are just some of what you'll see and smell at spice plantations in Kidichi on Zanzibar's main island, Unguja. You'll taste them, too, perhaps at food stalls in historic Stone Town. Here, coral-stone buildings with ornately carved doors are legacies of the Tanzanian archipelago's Arab and Indian spice traders. Offset the savory with the sugary sands of a palm-fringed beach. Hire a fishing boat on Matemwe and sail to Mnemba Island to snorkel among dolphins and turtles. Toast the turquoise Indian Ocean with a sundowner.

Zanzibar: spices at a market; Indian Ocean (right).

Temple Central

Strangler figs snake down crumbling stone from moss-coated roof tiles in the tiny courtyard of Ta Prohm temple. You savor the quiet—earlier, you were one of hundreds lining the moat opposite Angkor Wat, watching the dawn sky tint its conical towers pink. The crowds recalled a time, nine centuries ago, when Cambodia's enormous Angkor Archaeological Park was the Khmer capital—and the world's largest city. Today, its only permanent residents are set in stone: Bayon's huge faces, Angkor Wat's *apsaras* (nymphs), Angkor Thom's south gate statues. You hop a three-wheeled *tuk-tuk* back to Siem Reap for a different sort of people-watching, a meal at a café, and some time meditating on tomorrow's hopefully quiet return pilgrimage to Preah Khan and Neak Pean.

Cambodia: Vishnu statue in Angkor Wat (left);
Ta Prohm temple.

Island of the Gods

Bali's beaches are truly heavenly, but its spiritual vein runs far deeper—and well inland. A pilgrimage 3,000 feet up Gunung Agung, a sacred volcano, brings you to Pura Besakih, the Mother Temple complex of towering thatched shrines. Descend 300 stone steps through rice-paddy terraces to Pura Gunung Kawi, a valley temple with 25-foot shrines carved into rock and shrouded by jungle. In nearby Tampak Siring, bathe in sacred spring waters captured by ornate stone pools. Your soul sated, it's your body's turn. In Ubud, local produce is featured on menus at both cafés and spas. Book day treatments at Bali Botanica, or reach another level of bliss staying at resorts like Five Elements or COMO Shambhala.

Bali, Indonesia: Pura Besakih; rice paddies below
Gunung Agung volcano (right).

Australia's Red Center

Anangu belief holds that, during the Dreamtime, mythic beings created sacred landforms like the 1,142-foot plateau that is Uluru and the 36 domed rocks of Kata Tjuta amid the Valley of the Winds. In Uluru's cultural center and art galleries, Aboriginal Australia's unique world vision further unfolds in story and in works of dot art. As you hike around Uluru's 6-mile base or through the Valley of the Winds, your Anangu guide points out ancient rock paintings, hallowed watering holes, and significant plants. Around a campfire or at the Sounds of Silence restaurant, you sample bush tucker like kangaroo, emu, or even witchetty grubs. And, at dusk or dawn, you watch the sandstone heart of Aboriginal Australia turn deep red.

Northern Territory: Uluru (aka Ayers Rock) and ancient rock painting (left);
Valley of the Winds and Kata Tjuta (aka The Olgas) in Uluru-Kata Tjuta National Park.

Tasmanian Terroir

Ranchers, farmers, and vintners in Australia's southernmost state cherish the island's mild climate, clean air, and rich soil. Chefs and diners relish the resulting natural bounty at farm-to-fork restaurants like Stillwater and Black Cow Bistro in Launceston. North along the Tamar River, vineyards offer Tassie takes on cool-climate varietals—Pinot Noir at Sinapius, Riesling at Tamar Ridge, sparkling Chardonnay at Jansz. Other bottled delights include cider, beer, and whiskey. West of Launceston, the vistas of Cradle Mountain from Dove Lake are delectable. Trails here beckon you to walk off the fresh berries and artisanal cheeses you sampled at their sources along Highway 1 and the central northwest coast. You won't find such delicacies outside Tasmania, let alone the country: a good excuse for a second helping.

Australia: Dove Lake and Cradle Mountain (left); Pipers Brook Vineyard; a wallaby.

A Brazilian Gem

Time seems to have stopped in the town that gold built. Ouro Preto was the hub for the precious ore that poured from 18th-century mines in surrounding Minas Gerais. When the golden tide subsided, it left behind architectural treasures, like the baroque Nossa Senhora do Pilar church, with its gilt walls and ceilings. Steep, winding streets lined with colonial townhouses take you to Praça Tiradentes. Along the way, shop for the region's renowned gemstones, like imperial topaz, unique to Ouro Preto. Stop in restaurants and try *angu mineiro* and *tutu de feijão à mineira,* local takes on polenta and refried beans. The cuisine here is as rich and renowned as the history.

Ouro Preto: Nossa Senhora do Pilar church (left); scenic overview.

Timeless Uruguay

The Río de la Plata is so wide that even from atop Colonia del Sacramento's lighthouse you can barely see the opposite bank. A Portuguese warship slices through the chop under full sail, set on recapturing this beautiful and strategic town from the Spanish. You rub your eyes—it's just a ferry from Argentina. The time-travel sensation continues amid the Barrio Histórico's cobbled lanes and colonial houses. The river gives way to grasslands and vineyards out at a nearby *estancia* (ranch). During an *asado* (barbecue), a weather-worn gaucho pulls a knife from the waist of his baggy pants, leans over the glowing coals, and tends to the meat. You blink. He's still there. In this part of Uruguay, time really does seem to stand still.

Colonia del Sacramento: street scene (left);
gaucho tending a barbecue.

Coffee Country

You spoon lightly roasted, still-warm beans into the grinder and turn the crank. When you stay at a coffee hacienda in Colombia's Quindío region, brewing is a ritual to savor—the fitting end to the artisanal drying process you witnessed while wandering the plantation's muddy paths, stopping to finger green beans on the bush. The lush, cloud-topped slopes of the Corcora Valley are perfect for growing coffee—and for walking. In Los Nevados National Park, you hike among towering wax palms, cross rope bridges over rushing rivers, and spot toucans and hummingbirds. Their brilliant plumage is rivaled as much by the vibrantly painted balconies in sleepy Salento as by the tropical fruit awaiting you on the breakfast table . . . alongside that steaming cup of coffee.

Corcora Valley, Colombia

Mexico: restaurants in Oaxaca's *zócalo* (main square); chiles in a market (right).

Holy Mole!

You'd like to try the chile-fried *chapulines* (grasshoppers) sold in the Abastos Market, but your courage falters, so you sample another Oaxacan specialty instead. Cinnamon, cumin, cloves, pepper, bitter chocolate: It's hard to distinguish all the ingredients—more than 30, some say—that meld into the rich, dark *mole negro.* In restaurants like Pitiona and La Biznaga, cooking the sauce can take days. It takes years, though, to transform maguey plants into this southwestern Mexican region's famous mezcal. Small-batch vintages at Mezcalería los Amantes sear your throat and blow your mind. Equally mind altering? The pyramid-filled plateau of Monte Albán, once the Zapotec capital. Contemporary Zapotec and Mixtec crafts are among the eye-popping treasures in shops dotting Oaxaca's cobbled streets.

The Vines of Napa

There are myriad ways to sample Napa Valley's viticulture in a day—a good thing given this part of California has some 450 wineries! Consider a drive along the scenic Silverado Trail, between the towns of Napa and Calistoga, or a 36-mile jaunt on the Napa Valley Wine Train, with vineyard stops and gourmet, wine-paired meals served en route. You can also glimpse the valley from on high with a tram ride to the top of Sterling Vineyards, or descend into the wine caves of Stags' Leap Winery. Regardless of your choice, be sure to splurge on a memorable meal at one of famed-chef Thomas Keller's restaurants in bucolic Yountville, Napa Valley's hub.

Napa Valley, CA

Mission: Desert

Your mission, should you choose to accept it: explore the Sonora Desert around Old Pueblo (aka Tucson). You start at the 21-acre Arizona-Sonora Desert Museum, gathering intelligence on regional flora and fauna in its botanical garden and mini safari park. You reconnoiter desertscapes featuring 50-foot cacti in Saguaro National Park. You scout filmscapes at the Old Tucson Studios, whose storefronts appeared in *Rio Bravo*, *Tombstone*, and other great Westerns. Your next assignment? Investigate one of the exquisite 18th-century missions: San Xavier del Bac (code named White Dove of the Desert). After stealth explorations of Tucson's Barrio Viejo and El Presidio districts, you make a speedy getaway north, up Mount Lemmon Highway, to your safe house: the Miraval Arizona Resort & Spa, a true Sonoran sanctuary.

Around Tuscon, AZ: Sonora desertscape;
San Xavier del Bac Mission (right).

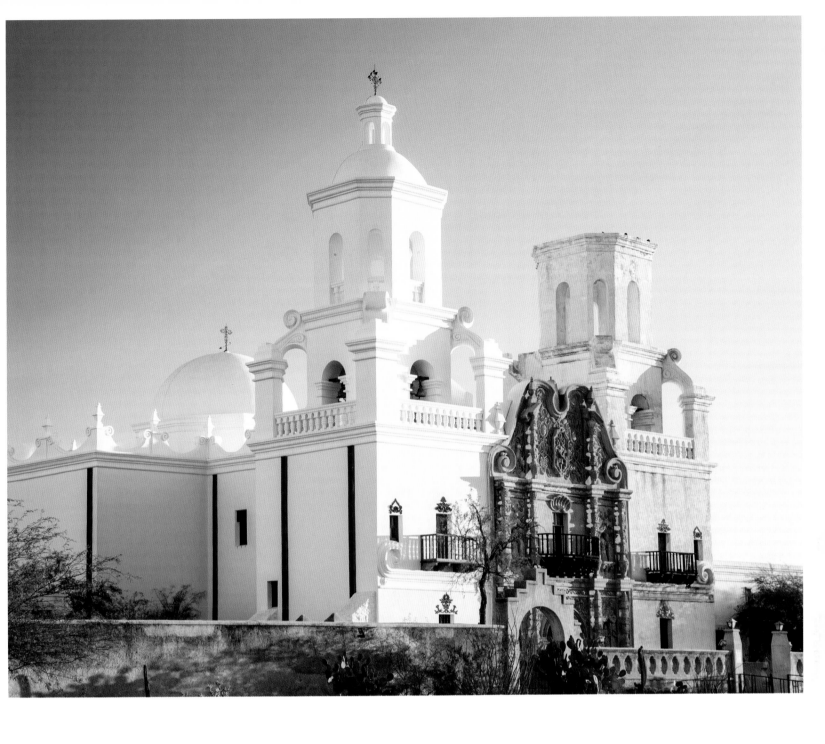

Canyon de Chelly National Monument, AZ

The Heart of Navajo Nation

You descend into an ancient sandstone canyon that's been continuously inhabited for nearly 5,000 years. You gaze up at the 800-foot-high, pencil-thin Spider Rock, the home to Spider Woman, a Navajo deity. Nearby are the ancient pueblo ruins of Mummy Cave and Antelope House, built by the Anasazi in this corner of Arizona over 1,000 years ago. Is there any doubt that you're within Canyon de Chelly, in the heart of the 27,000-square mile Navajo Nation? Local Native American guides help you learn more about the landmarks and legends of this sacred site. At the end of the day, pick up some fry bread and tacos at the Junction Restaurant in Chinle—one of The Nation's administrative centers—before spending the night at the Thunderbird Lodge.

Adobe buildings on Canyon Road, Santa Fe.

The Art of the Canyon

The weather is crisp, the sky a cobalt blue of the type Georgia O'Keeffe used in her paintings. It's the perfect day for an art walk, so you wander in and out of Canyon Road's 50 or so adobe-clad galleries taking in the Native American, Southwestern, and contemporary works. You stay fortified with a cup of piñon coffee and a pastry from Caffe Greco or some fiery cuisine at The Compound. Welcome to Santa Fe, the jewel-like capital of New Mexico, where you soon discover that Canyon Road's artistic beauty is matched by that of the Historic Plaza—and by the sun setting over all of this magical city, a sight best enjoyed with cocktails on the roof deck at La Fonda Hotel.

On Sacred Ground

Small fires burn in ancient hearths. Dogs wander through courtyards and drink from the Rio Pueblo. Tour groups led by local guides softly shuffle into a Mission-style chapel. Workers patch a cracked adobe wall. A shopkeeper opens a door, and the unmistakable smell of freshly made fry bread hits your nostrils. Native Americans have called Taos Pueblo home for nearly 1,000 years, making it the nation's oldest continuously inhabited community. Unless it's closed for ceremonial observances, a stop at this UNESCO World Heritage Site at the base of Wheeler Peak— New Mexico's highest at over 13,000 feet—isn't to be missed. This is life. This is Taos Pueblo.

Taos Pueblo, NM

Cliff Dwellings of the Ancients

Say it's 800 years ago. You're a young Anasazi following a well-trodden mesa path, carrying water from a stream back to your home—Cliff Palace, a 150-room sandstone-and-mortar structure tucked elegantly beneath a rock outcropping. Fast-forward to today. You can still take that mesa path to Cliff Palace, one of 4,000 sites to explore in Colorado's Mesa Verde National Park, a UNESCO World Heritage Site and the nation's largest archaeological preserve. Tours of Cliff Palace and the Long House, each of which housed over 100 people, bring the culture of these master builders to life. The Anasazi might have mysteriously left—perhaps due to a prolonged drought—after 1300 AD or so, but their dwellings have been miraculously preserved.

Cliff palace (near and far), Mesa Verde National Park, CO

Cowboy Culture

Ready for a Texas town with the biggest—and best—split personality in the country? Look no further than Fort Worth. By day, you can watch a cattle drive through the Stockyards National Historic District or tour the National Cowgirl Hall of Fame before a stroll through Tadao Ando's Modern Art Museum or Louis Kahn's equally sublime Kimbell Art Museum. The Philip Johnson–designed Amon Carter Museum of American Art is as renowned for its Remingtons and Russells as for its 20th-century photography archive. At night, swap highbrow for honky-tonk yet again with some two-stepping or bull riding at Billy Bob's, or grab a thick, juicy steak at Del Frisco's Double Eagle, amid the bright lights of Sundance Square.

Fort Worth, TX: Stockyards (left); Modern Art Museum.

Art for Artists

A dream in a desert landscape—that was the vision of artist and sculptor Donald Judd, a master of 20th-century minimalism. And when you make it all the way out to Marfa—some 200 miles from El Paso and 500 miles from Dallas—you'll see just how well his exquisitely constructed steel and plywood "boxes" mesh with the windswept West Texas landscape. Both the Chinati and Judd foundations have collected and preserved hundreds of works by Judd as well as by light master Dan Flavin, steel bender John Chamberlain, and dozens of others. East of town, on Route 67, you might get a glimpse of the mysterious Marfa Lights; northwest of town, off Highway 90 near Valentine, you'll definitely see the quirky Prada Marfa installation.

Around Marfa, TX: Prada Marfa art installation near the town of Valentine; a desertscape (right).

Tracing the South

You wandered amid wisteria and tulips in Monmouth Historic Inn's enormous garden, studied the unfinished cupola of octagonal Longwood House, and explored the stately interiors of Stanton Hall and Melrose. You sipped champagne from a rocking chair on the porch of Dunleith, and visited the home of William Johnson, a freed slave who became a barber and landlord in the 1830s. This is antebellum history at its finest. This is Natchez, Mississippi, the southern terminus of the famous Natchez Trace. Touring its many well-preserved estates gave you a taste of its living, breathing Southern charm. Hungry for more, though, you settle in for grilled oysters at Roux 61 or cocktails and a petite filet at Kings Tavern—followed by a sunset stroll along the Mississippi River.

Natchez, MS: Stanton Hall (left); twilight on the Mississippi River.

A Day at the Races

Amid rolling bluegrass hills just outside of Lexington, Kentucky, you hear the muffled thud of hooves as Thoroughbreds are put through their paces. Watching the daybreak workout at Keeneland Race Track, a National Historic Landmark, leaves you breathless: Some of these majestic creatures are being trained for a run at glory in the Kentucky Derby or the Breeders' Cup. After rubbing elbows with breeders, trainers, and jockeys during breakfast at the Track Kitchen, you head to the Kentucky Horse Park. Here, you immerse yourself in all things equine by touring the International Museum of the Horse, catching one of the daily horse shows—or going riding yourself—and shopping for equine-themed gifts. End your day admiring the powerful, life-size sculptures at Lexington's Thoroughbred Park.

Lexington, KY: Kentucky Horse Park (left); Keeneland Race Track.

Confluence of History

Thomas Jefferson described the meeting point of two deep gorges, cut by the Potomac and Shenandoah rivers, as ". . . one of the most stupendous scenes in nature." The village of Harpers Ferry sits at this very junction—and that of West Virginia, Virginia, and Maryland. Get steeped in abolitionist history at John Brown's Fort, and walk the cobbled streets of the Harpers Ferry National Historical Park. Learn how the town changed hands eight times during the Civil War and how it evolved into a transit hub on both the C&O Canal and the B&O Railroad. Climb Jefferson's Rock to see the whole of Harpers Ferry and its stupendous setting for yourself.

Harpers Ferry, WV

The Gilded Age

Gazing up at the grand staircase inside the Italian palazzo–style Breakers, you picture Cornelius Vanderbilt II descending, en route to the ballroom or an outing on the water. Yes, the insanely wealthy have "outings." They also call their summer manses "cottages." In Newport, Rhode Island, stunning excesses of Gilded Age wealth are set in stone by design . . . of famous American architects, that is. Leafy Bellevue Avenue takes you to Beaux Arts–style Marble House (like The Breakers, designed by Richard Morris Hunt for a Vanderbilt) and Rosecliff (by Stanford White for a Nevada silver heiress). More "modest" wooden manors include the rambling, Shingle-style Isaac Bell House and Gothic Revival Kingscote. All are impeccably designed and perfectly aligned cliffside, overlooking the sea.

Rosecliff Mansion, Newport, RI

The Shaker Life

Only gently rustling trees break the hush in Shaker Village. Amid almost 700 pastoral acres in Canterbury, New Hampshire, whitewashed fences line grassy laneways connecting the 30 historic structures. A soft-spoken docent leads you through tidy workshops and ship-shape rooms. Wide-planked floors and chests of drawers emit the sweet smell of vintage wood. Shelves are stocked with well-ordered jars of dried herbs; walls are hung with Shaker-designed corn brooms, ladder-back chairs (upside-down, so the seats don't get dusty), tools, and straw bonnets. It's as if the brothers and sisters have just left to attend chores elsewhere. After all, "Hands to Work, Hearts to God." The devout Shakers who once lived here are indeed gone, but their industrious ideals, ingenious designs, and elegant craftsmanship live on.

Shaker Village, Canterbury, NH: vegetable garden (top left); the meetinghouse (bottom left); interior scene.

Lobster on the Dock

It's early in the morning. Seagulls cry as fishermen unload the day's catch. The smell of hot coffee and fresh donuts emanates from diners and cafés. You're in a small fishing village somewhere, right? Nope. You're actually in Maine's capital, Portland—a fabulous base from which to explore the endless coves and jutting peninsulas of Vacationland's 3,500-mile coast. Just be sure to spend some time in the city itself. Head out for a stroll and some shopping along the Old Port's cobblestone streets. Sample offerings from one of a dozen or so microbreweries, and tuck in to the wood oven–roasted catch of the day at Fore Street or some lobster, steamed right on the dock, from J's Oyster.

Maine coast near Portland: Portland Head Lighthouse, Cape Elizabeth, ME (left); fishing and lobster boats.

Blissful Retreats

"On earth there is no heaven, but there are pieces of it."
—*Jules Renard*

Bora Bora, French Polynesia

The Matterhorn, Switzerland

True Alpine Paradise

A ring of Alps and plenty of pistes? Check and check. The 38 peaks surrounding Zermatt include the magnificent, twisted Matterhorn. The 200 miles of runs spill over from Switzerland into Italy. There's also mountaineering, snowshoeing or hiking, and weighing up which watch to buy from the Bahnhofstrasse boutiques. Wooden ski chalets? Check. Icicles hang from their eaves in winter, flowers pour from their window boxes in summer. Great food? Check. A hundred or so eateries serve up everything from take-out to top-tier. Swiss spas? Yet another check. The setting is rustic at the Alpenhof; sleek at the Backstage Vernissage; and inspirational at the Omnia, whose plunge pool has Matterhorn views. The verdict is clear: Zermatt ticks all the Alpine-paradise boxes.

La Dolce Vita

A steep, cobbled alley opens onto a small piazza flanked by sparkling Lake Orta, one of the lesser-known bodies of water in northern Italy's justly famous Lake District. Of course, you won't neglect the grandes dames: Lugano, Como, Garda, and Maggiore. But your approach to lake-hopping is whimsical. First, you rent a convertible—maybe even a vintage one—and enjoy fancy-free waterside drives. Next, you buy an all-day ferry pass and ply the waters, passing shores dotted with pastel-painted villas, ornamental gardens, monasteries housing boutique hotels, and churches carved straight into the rock face. You disembark from time to time, confident of finding stunning scenery, great shopping, classic food and wine, and strong espresso in every sweet little lakeside village and town.

Italian Lake District: Baveno on Lake Maggiore;
Torno on Lake Como (right).

Forged by Fire

The sun sinks behind the caldera like an ember, igniting the sky crimson and the water deep orange. The fiery end to each Santorini day is a fitting tribute to the massive volcanic eruption that formed this Greek archipelago. The volcano shaped and colored your day, too. You visited the ash-preserved ruins of the Bronze Age Akrotiri settlement, sampled bright-red Santorini tomatoes and sweet amber *vin santo*, and lounged on the pink-red sands of Kokkini Beach. But, like the volcano, you take time to rest. You're back at cliff-top Imerovigli village, crisply painted in white and blue. At cave-house hotels here and in Oia, rooms hewn into the rock provide cool and luxurious shelter, while infinity pools reflect the sunset's fire.

Santorini, Greece

Thai Hill Country

Legend holds that the Lanna kings of northern Thailand's Chiang Mai Province relied on a white elephant carrying a relic of the Buddha to choose the site for the magnificent Wat Phrathat Doi Suthep. You reach the copper-clad *chedi* (reliquary tower) of the 14th-century temple complex via its 300 steps or its tram. Beyond is the 5,500-foot, cloud-shrouded Doi Suthep mountain. You'll return to explore caves and waterfalls in its national park before heading farther into the hills to a tribal village or an elephant sanctuary. Below is Chiang Mai, where you've shopped along fashionable Nimmahaemin Road, sampled spicy street food, and had your cares rubbed away with a day-spa Thai massage or a full day's indulgence at the Four Seasons or Dhara Dhevi resorts.

Wat Phrathat Doi Suthep—inside and out.

Marine Metropolis

A neon-yellow butterfly fish darts past your mask, followed by a school of electric-blue surgeonfish. A shadow passes as a reef shark glides overhead. It's like a Times Square of the deep, where you're a tourist amidst marine residents who dart purposefully around towers of coral, their suits cut from absurdly flashy cloth. Poolside at your hotel on Hamilton Island, the largest of Australia's Whitsundays, fellow guests bait you with suggestions: hit the brilliant-white sands of Whitehaven Beach and snorkel with turtles, game fish from a charter yacht, cay-hop on a live-aboard dive boat, escape to private islets like Lizard or Haggerstone. With 2,900 reefs and 900 islands, there's enough Great Barrier Reef to keep you busy for several lifetimes.

Queensland, Australia: Great Barrier Reef.

A South Pacific Jewel

Turquoise and aquamarine: The lagoon shimmers beneath the stilts of your thatched cabin—perhaps at the Four Seasons, St. Regis, or Le Meridien. In Bora Bora, it's hard to stay anywhere *but* over the water. Sapphire: Taking to deeper blue waters beyond the *motus* (atolls), you dive or snorkel among turtles or even sharks. Emerald: Two verdant peaks, Otemanu and Pahia, rise up on the main island. You explore one for a bird's-eye view of paradise. Black pearls: At the Bora Pearl Company Farm, you learn about these unique Tahitian treasures, dive for an oyster, or design your own jewelry. Diamonds and gold: Glinting ring fingers and loving gazes reveal the reason most guests splurge on this gem of an island.

Bora Bora, French Polynesia

Maui, HI

A Hawaiian Paradise

Maui is truly a blissful American escape: pristine and exotic yet still on home soil, even if it is of the volcanic variety on an island 2,000 miles west of California. It's Hawaii in a microcosm: unspoiled shores, killer snorkeling and scuba diving, a lush interior with fields of taro and sugarcane and a mountainous backdrop. West Maui's beaches are the settings for some of the world's most perfect resorts and the launching point for watery excursions to the submerged Molokini Crater. On the east coast, the winding drive to Hana from Kahului snakes through lush forests and along craggy coasts. And the views from Haleakalā National Park, home to the island's 10,000-foot volcano, give you a sense of it all.

Pacific Ocean Blue

Avalon. In Arthurian legend, it's the mythic island where the sword, Excalibur, was forged. You recall this as your ferry approaches California's Santa Catalina Island. Then, your jaw drops at the mythic, ocean-blue beauty of the setting—graceful, horseshoe-shaped Avalon Bay, the boats of all sizes bobbing in the marina, the town of Avalon climbing the hills just up from the beach, the curved majesty of the Art Deco Catalina Casino jutting out from Casino Point, and water so clear you can spot fish and coral from the ferry deck. Don't forget to disembark, though—the island's windswept hills, roaming bison, unparalleled snorkeling, uber-fresh seafood, refreshing spa treatments, and soft beds await. If this is the stuff of legend, then to heck with reality.

Views of Avalon Bay, Catalina Island, CA

Mendocino Mornings

It's just after dawn in Mendocino. Mist still blankets this small Victorian town, a quiet aerie overlooking the Pacific. You enjoy breakfast at your B&B, one of about two dozen here, and then don a light sweater and head out. Warmed by a second cup of coffee from Moody's, you walk the trail to Big River Beach in Mendocino Headlands State Park. Waves crash on the craggy coast as the California sun burns off the mist. The Gallery Bookshop opens, and you browse the shelves until it's time for another meal, perhaps at Café Beaujolais or Patterson's Pub. The rest of the day—with a spa treatment at the Stanford Inn or some whale-watching off the coast—will go equally well. We promise.

Mendocino Headlands State Park and Point Cabrillo
Light Station (left); running along the California coast.

Lavender fields, Sequim, WA

Purple Fields of Majesty

Once in a while, nature and culture meet in a blaze of glory. The incredible aroma and stunning color produced by endless rows of lavender in Washington State's Dungeness River valley perfectly complement the region's artisanal shops and restaurants. In summer, the Sequim Lavender Festival and Farm Tour is a distillation of it all. Shop for herb-laced products or groove to bands at farms like Olympic Lavender, Purple Haze, Sunshine Herb & Lavender, or Jardin du Soleil. Dine on that famous Dungeness crab at Dockside Grill on Sequim Bay. Jutting out into the Strait of Juan de Fuca, the Dungeness National Wildlife Refuge—home to eagles, harbor seals, and black-tailed deer—is yet another of this lush valley's year-round wonders.

Escape Across the Water

The ferry winds its way from Anacortes, 80 miles north of Seattle, through evergreen-draped islands shrouded by Puget Sound fog. Up ahead, the lights of Friday Harbor pierce the mist. The ferry docks—and Washington State's San Juan Archipelago, with some 400 islands, is yours to explore. On Lopez Island, you can relax at the Edenwild Inn before heading out on a tour to spot whales off the coast. Head up to Orcas Island for a hike through the pines at Moran State Park and a taste of Rip Tide Porter from Island Hoppin' Brewery. Or just stay put in Friday Harbor, with a room overlooking the docks at the Island Inn and a feast of pan-seared scallops at the Backdoor Kitchen. Escape, indeed.

San Juan Islands, WA: killer whale and Friday Harbor; kayaker at Vendovi Island (right).

A Natural High

The trees fly past. You're slaloming over thick Canadian powder through the pines on Bark Sandwich, one of over 200 ski runs at British Columbia's twin-peaked Whistler Blackcomb resort. Or you're whizzing along a zip line, high above Fitzsimmons Creek, or careening round a cambered bend on Dirt Merchant, one of many mountain-bike runs. Maybe you're aboard the Peak 2 Peak Gondola: The world's longest and highest free-span lift carries skiers in winter and hikers and bikers in summer. Or perhaps you're kayaking or rafting the area's many watercourses, passing within spitting distance of foraging black bears. Finally, the trees stand still. But, as you plunge into successive outdoor baths at the Scandinave spa, you realize that in Whistler, even downtime can have your heart pumping.

Whistler Blackcomb Mountain, British Columbia, Canada

Aurora borealis, Fairbanks, AK

An Alaskan Aurora

It's 10 degrees Fahrenheit, but you're in a bathing suit. Ice crystals are forming in your hair, but the rest of your body is submerged in hot, steaming water. Sheets of eerie greenish light pulsate in the pitch-black sky above. This is Chena Hot Springs, 60 miles northeast of Fairbanks. On any given night, people from across the globe soak in these springs—and soak up the show. Although the almost-nightly aurora borealis display is best in winter, its only-in-Alaska quirk is always matched by that of this resort, founded some 100 years ago by entrepreneurs. Warmed by your soak, you chill out in the Ice Museum and its Aurora Ice Bar, both handcrafted by local ice sculptors and both very cool.

Oasis of Chic

Past the bumper-to-bumper traffic of Los Angeles, past the bedroom communities and strip malls of San Bernardino County, past the sprawling arrays of windmills generating electric power, lies a retro-chic oasis in the desert: Palm Springs. This is where Angelenos come to zone out from their hectic lives, whether that means a spa treatment at the Parker or a poolside nap at the Palm Springs Hotel. The arid landscape does beckon—with a hike through massive palm trees in nearby Palm Canyon and an aerial tram ride to the top of San Jacinto Mountain. But so does in-town shopping for modernist treasures. And you can't go wrong with brunch at Cheeky's and a few Poison Darts at Bootlegger Tiki.

Cities of Desert Hot Springs and Palm Springs, CA (left);
a desert garden.

A House on the Lake

It's just after dawn. The Arizona sun peers from behind a sandstone mesa, lighting up the rich red cliffs surrounding Lake Powell's glassy, placid waters. You switch on the houseboat's coffeemaker. Enjoy the solitude. Before you finish your first cup, everyone else will be awake, eager to dive sternward for a swim or to go waterskiing. And that's only morning on the country's second-largest man-made reservoir, created by the 700-foot Glen Canyon Dam. Later, there might be a hike to Rainbow Bridge, a sacred Navajo site, or some bass fishing for the evening's dinner. At sunset, settle in with a nightcap, and prepare for the sight of a million stars above a (once again) quiet lake.

Lake Powell, AZ

Red Rock West

The sun sets over Sedona, Arizona. From the patio of L'Auberge de Sedona, you reflect on the harmonic convergence that was your day. What happened? Maybe you took a sunrise hike to Cathedral Rock or Devil's Bridge, followed by some yoga or a round of golf. Perhaps you paused to meditate at the Chapel of the Holy Cross, embedded in sandstone outside town. Or maybe you explored ancient cliff dwellings at Honanki Heritage Site or Montezuma Castle National Monument. Later, you might have made your way up to Oak Creek Canyon or Schnebly Hill Road for panoramic afternoon views. As night falls, you ponder Sedona's quintessential draws—saturated red rocks, brilliant blue sky, and utter serenity.

Around Sedona, AZ: red rock country horseback riding; formation views near Schnebly Hill Road (right).

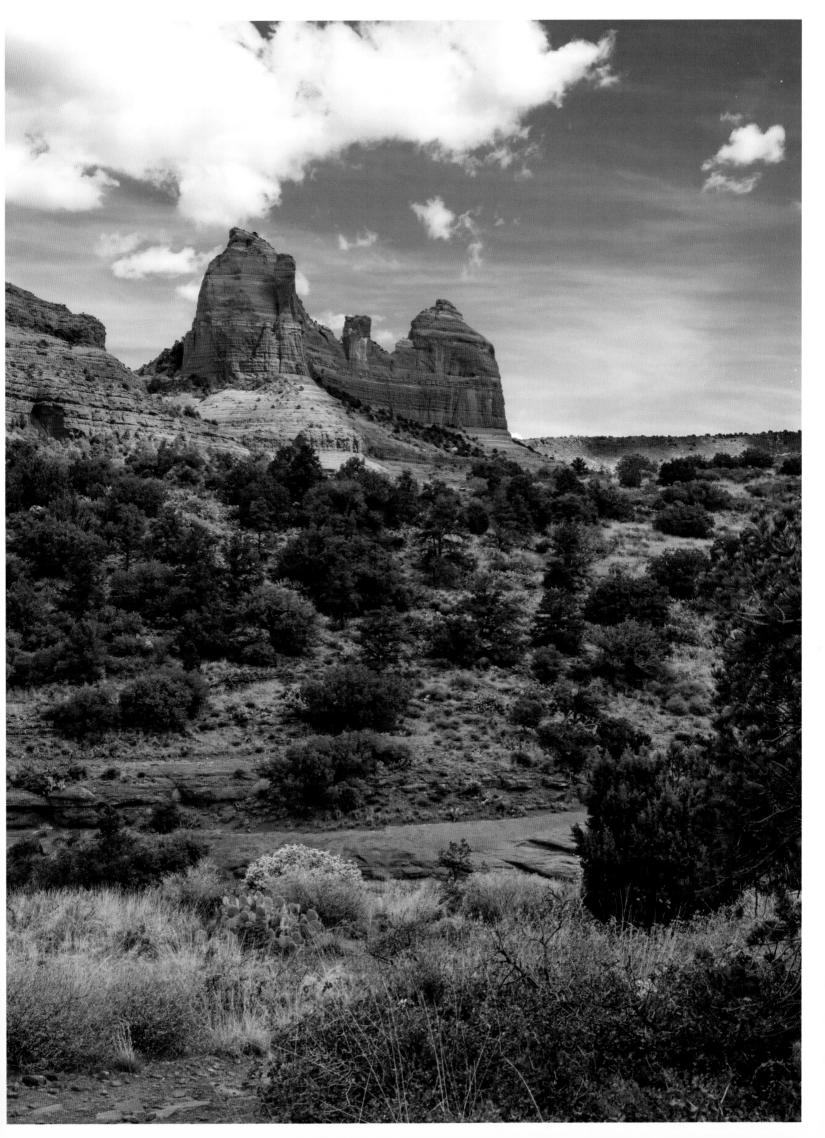

Rocky Mountain Warmth

You're footsore, grimy, and tired after a full day (or maybe even a full week) of hiking through the majestic Rockies. Twenty minutes later, you're soaking in an equally majestic outdoor pool—in the shadow of those very same mountains—waiting for your massage to begin. This is the pure heaven of Glenwood Hot Springs, a vast Colorado complex of warm springs and caverns (not to mention soft beds) that's been relaxing visitors since 1888. After a restful night, you even feel good enough to get back out there, perhaps on a hike to the secluded pool of Hanging Lake or some caving, mountain biking, or zip-lining in Glenwood Canyon . . . with yet another soak or spa treatment waiting when you're done.

Hanging Lake and Rock Spout Park (top left); South Canyon Creek near Glenwood Springs, CO (top right); Glenwood Hot Springs Resort (bottom right).

Skiing the Aspen Way

The sunrise slowly illuminates the 14,000-foot Maroon Bells, snowcapped twin peaks in the Colorado Rockies. It's a signal: Time to hit the back bowls of Aspen Highlands, the 3-mile run at Aspen Mountain, the terrain park at Buttermilk, or the 94 trails at Snowmass. Where to begin? The answer is simple: Stay long enough to touch all the bases, including the gaily lit town of Aspen itself. After time on the slopes, stroll through exhibits at the postmodern Aspen Art Museum, grab a brew (or two) at HOPS Culture, and tuck into some risotto or a rib-eye at Wild Fig. It's all part of what makes Aspen special, both day and night.

Aspen, CO

The Island That Time Forgot

No driveways. Of all the Mackinac Island trivia, this bit is probably the quirkiest. Why no driveways? The Michigan island in Lake Huron is blissfully free of all motorized vehicles (they startle the horses, ya know). So it's a carriage ride between the ferry and your hotel and then another to the Victorian-studded Main Street to hit the fudge shops or cozy pubs. You can also hike and bike here, perhaps through Mackinac Island State Park and to its famous fort overlooking the stunning harbor. Leisurely pursuits include tucking into schnitzel and spätzle at the Woods Restaurant or hanging out on the Grand Hotel's enormous porch (660 feet, dozens of rocking chairs). Chances of missing your car? Zero.

Mackinac Island, MI

Victorians by the Beach

Life in Cape May: sitting in a rocking chair on the porch of your grand Victorian hotel—or small Victorian B&B—sipping a cup of morning tea. The ocean breeze and tang of the salty air remind you that you're far from the hustle and bustle of the New York metropolitan area. Charmingly situated just beyond Exit 0 off New Jersey's Garden State Parkway, Cape May is the state's southernmost point, decked out with beaches, marshes, wildlife preserves, wineries, and more Victorian and bungalow architecture than any town 10 times its size. Climb the 199 steps to the top of Cape May Lighthouse for a bird's-eye view of it all, or just laze on the beach between seafood feasts at the Pier House.

Cape May, NJ

New England, Personified

When you descend into the snow-covered valley, where Stowe sits nestled amid the Green Mountains of Vermont, one image leaps to mind: *New England Winter Scene* by Currier & Ives. This picture-postcard village, complete with white church steeples and red barns, is only lacking a parade of horse-drawn sleighs to send you back a century or so. No matter the season, Stowe's gaily lit shops and restaurants are picturesque against the mountain backdrop. In summer and fall, events such as the Stoweflake Balloon Festival and the Foliage Arts Festival rule the day. But the town really picks up for January's Winter Carnival, whose merrymakers join the masses of skiers slicing down the slopes of Stowe Mountain and Smuggler's Notch resorts.

Stowe, VT

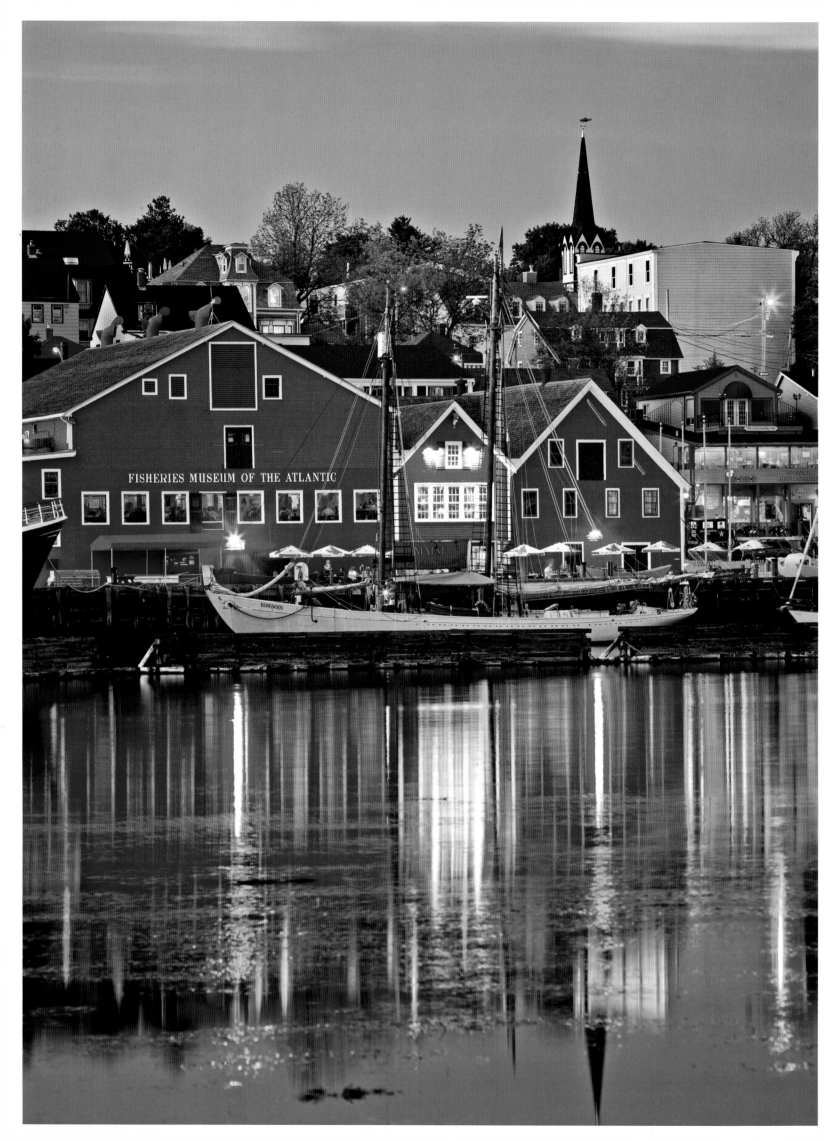

Canadian Coastal Inspiration

As the tidal bore rushes Burncoat Head in the Bay of Fundy, you see why Nova Scotia's coast so captivated poets like William Carlos Williams and Elizabeth Bishop. The scene is equally lyrical two hours south, in the one-time shipbuilding town of Lunenburg. Colorful old houses line its waterfront, and the *Bluenose II,* a replica of the schooner on the Canadian dime, is moored at its wharf. You experience poetry in motion during a harbor sail and find genius in the vodka samples at the Ironworks Distillery. Ensconced at the Lennox Inn 1791, you dream of the day's maritime adventures and those to come. In the morning, you head east to the fishing village of Blue Rocks for yet another tide of inspiration.

Nova Scotia: town of Lunenburg (left); the *Bluenose II.*

Shelling in Sanibel

Glittering waters wash flotsam and jetsam ashore all along the Gulf of Mexico. But Sanibel Island is the gulf's "Capital of Shells." You'll need a nice long back massage from one of its beachside resorts after a day out hunting for those elaborate, twisty whelks or those classic, sonorous conchs. Most of the time, the South Florida sun will be high in the sky as you comb for natural treasures—or snorkel, scuba dive, golf, or play tennis. On the rare rainy day, the collections at the Bailey-Matthews National Shell Museum won't disappoint.

Sanibel Island, FL

Islands in the Dream

Wear sunglasses or squint. Those are your options on the powdery white sands of Magens Bay, gazing out at the calm, sunlit, electric-blue water. Trips to equally stunning Lindquist Beach and Secret Harbour confirm it: St. Thomas is one of those island paradises that everyone dreams of. And the dream continues—while touring Charlotte Amalie, with its cheerily painted colonial architecture, or on a day trip to St. John's island for some hiking or bird-watching in Virgin Islands National Park. The food is dreamy everywhere, from simple conch fritters at a beach shack to a gourmet French-Caribbean experience at the Old Stone Farmhouse. And whether you've booked a small cottage in town or a suite at the Ritz-Carlton, you realize one simple fact: You're in paradise.

St. Thomas, USVI: dreamy waters (top left and right);
Charlotte Amalie (bottom left).

Caribbean Immersion

From Anse Chastanet's silver sands, you wade into the warm Caribbean and toy with a full submersion to explore the offshore reef. To the south, St. Lucia's iconic twin peaks rise sharply from the sea—yesterday, you immersed yourself in dense forest while hiking Gros Piton, the larger of the two. At the Boucan Hotel, in the hills south of Soufrière, you plan to immerse yourself in chocolate: metaphorically, on a tour of the surrounding cocoa plantation and by making your own chocolate bar, and literally, with a full-body cacao wrap (perhaps while sampling estate-made truffles). Ultimately, though, you plunge into fitness and well being at The BodyHoliday, an all-inclusive resort near Castries, where offerings include workout classes, archery, yoga, and a daily spa treatment.

St. Lucia: Two Pitons (left); Caribbean reef.

The Glowing Bays of Puerto Rico

It's a moonless night. You're paddling through a mangrove swamp, your only source of illumination the tiny lights aboard your kayak and others around you. As you emerge from the swamp into a wide, dark bay, things brighten for a moment. Blue-green sparkles trail along in the ripples of your paddle strokes. You get the same mystical effect passing your hand through the water. Glowing water droplets fall from your fingertips as well. Although it seems like pixie magic, it's actually caused by an unusual type of plankton known as bioluminescent dinoflagellates. In the bio bays of Laguna Grande, off Puerto Rico's northeast coast, and Mosquito Bay, off the laid-back islet of Vieques, nature is pure alchemy.

Beach (left) and fishing boats, Vieques Island, Puerto Rico

Blue Mountain Hideaway

The weather is sweet, though steamy, as you depart Kingston along the winding Irish Town Road. You're bound for the cooler climes of Jamaica's Blue Mountains and a stay in a colonial-style cottage at Strawberry Hill Hotel, owned by Island Records founder Chris Blackwell. In the 1970s, the label's best-known artist, Bob Marley, was a frequent guest. Today, some of the world's best-known coffee grows on the surrounding slopes: You might stir some of it up on an estate tour, with a sample at the roadside EITS Café, or with a coffee scrub at the hotel spa. You might also hike along trails through the lush landscape and to secluded waterfalls. Regardless, you'll remain hidden amid mountains bathed in their namesake color.

Jamaica's Blue Mountains: Strawberry Hill Hotel and coffee beans; forest (right).

Belize by Boat

Above you are a thousand stars; around you, the gently lapping Caribbean. To your aft, laid-back Caye Caulker, where you lounged under palms and feasted on lobster before boarding your catamaran. Forward is the Belize Barrier Reef: miles of crystal waters, dotted with sandy cayes and prime diving, snorkeling, and fishing spots. Dolphins and manatees swim amid mangrove-fringed Turneffe Atoll; you swim through coral formations and gaze (or dive yet again) into the 400-foot-deep Great Blue Hole at Lighthouse Reef. Your southernmost stop is the fishing paradise of Glover's Reef. Nearby, the seabed plunges hundreds of feet, making for still more dramatic dives. Why more people don't simply sail off into Belize remains a mystery—one for which you're grateful.

Glover's Reef; Great Blue Hole (right).

Under the Maya Sun

Dawn breaks as you push off the powdery sand, finishing your last sun salutation below the ruins in Tulum. True, the ancient Maya venerated the sun differently, but in this boho beach town, you'll hear "*namaste*" as often as "*adiós.*" After more prosaic seaside solar worship, you climb closer to the heavens at the pyramid in nearby Coba. The Maya also held cenotes sacred as underworld portals: The sun lights up one cool turquoise pool at Cenote Dos Ojos, but you need a flashlight and diving gear to see stalactites in the other's depths. Boating the mangroves of the Sian Ka'an Biosphere Reserve, you spot crocodiles, manatees, turtles, howler monkeys . . . every creature under the Maya sun—or so it feels.

Mexico's Yucatán Peninsula: Nohoch Mul Temple, Coba, and Maya carving; ruins at Tulum (right).

Eco-Luxe

Cloud forests, rain forests, volcanic highlands, cattle-filled plains, and coasts both Pacific and Caribbean—peaceful Costa Rica has a rich wardrobe of natural looks. You can try each on for size at accommodations where style is seamlessly sewn to sustainability. Howler monkeys and scarlet macaws are fellow guests at Lapa Rios, an eco-lodge in its own 1,000-acre reserve in the Pacific southeast. At the Almonds and Corals Hotel, wooden boardwalks lead from your bungalow through the rain forest to a Caribbean beach that's private—except for the leatherback turtles, that is. In the central highlands, coffee and cacao farms surround Finca Rosa Blanca. Here you can hike the smoking Poás Volcano, raft the Pacuare River, or seek calmer waters in the infinity pool.

Costa Rica's Pacuare River; La Paz waterfall gardens near
Poás Volcano National Park (right).

Wilder Endeavors

"There is pleasure in the pathless woods,
There is rapture in the lonely shore,
There is society where none intrudes,
By the deep sea, and music in its roar:
I love not Man the less, but Nature more. . ."
—*Lord Byron*

Joshua Tree National Park, CA

The Earth Performs

The rocks crack. For millennia, tectonic plates have separated to create a dramatic rocky rift through Thingvellir National Park, just east of Reykjavik on Iceland's Golden Circle route. But for centuries, the site has united Icelanders: The world's oldest parliament began here around 930 AD. The steam gushes. Every few minutes, the Strokkur Geyser erupts from the gurgling mud of the Haukadalur geothermal field. The water crashes. At Gulfoss, the Hvítá River tumbles down ledges and into a deep crevice. The crater yawns. The Kerith Volcano is dormant, but its last eruption left a massive red-rock caldera cupping a vivid blue pool. Your muscles relax. The geothermal waters and silica-rich mud treatments at the Blue Lagoon spa are welcome after so much geological drama.

Thingvellir National Park, Iceland

Komodo National Park, Indonesia

Here Be Dragons

"Stick together, and don't leave the path," your guide says as you step off the pier. You're happy to oblige—especially upon spotting your first Komodo dragon. The 10-foot, fearsome but fascinating lizard approaches, clawed feet clicking, forked tongue flicking. Only about 5,000 of these Jurassic giants remain on the Indonesian islands of Komodo and Rinca. The waters here are equally exotic: They shimmer with nocturnal phosphorescence, caused by bioluminescent phytoplankton, and contain over 1,000 species of fish and 350 species of coral—but relatively few divers. Some have booked into a relaxed hotel edging Komodo National Park. But you've decided that a traditional, wooden, two-masted *phinisi*, transformed into a live-aboard dive boat, makes a much more fitting base for exploring the land of dragons.

Maasai Mara in Motion

Hundreds of thousands of wildebeest move in choreographed unison. It's just one of many dances during the annual migration across the Serengeti. In the grass and scrub, cheetahs, lions, and hyenas are poised to leap. From the safety of your vehicle, you glimpse them—or maybe graceful giraffes and zebra or lumbering rhinos, elephants, and hippos. It's Africa in motion, a safari dream come true. And the dream continues in your camp, set on conservancy land immediately north of Kenya's Maasai Mara National Reserve and leased from Maasai communities. Some of the tiny camps here are luxurious, others more rustic. All, however, are surrounded by hundreds of acres of savanna, with nothing but canvas between you and the ballet of clouds in the African sky.

Maasai Mara National Reserve, Kenya

The Smoke That Thunders

The drizzle turns to spray and the roar becomes thunderous as you emerge from the rain-forest footpath onto the rock platform. Victoria Falls plunge 350 feet into a 5,600-foot-wide chasm straddling the Zimbabwe–Zambia border. One cascade, two countries, multiple choices. The view from Zambia is up close and thrilling. That from Zimbabwe is panoramic. You can briefly transcend boundaries on helicopter tours or leisurely river cruises. You can canoe above the falls and run rapids below them. The intrepid rappel down into the gorge or bungee-jump off Victoria Falls Bridge. The less daring are content to enjoy the smoke-like mist during afternoon tea on the veranda of the Victoria Falls Hotel.

Zimbabwe–Zambia: Victoria Falls; white water rafting on the Zambesi River at the Victoria Falls Bridge, Zambia side (right).

A Thirst for Namibia

The 900-year-old camel thorn trees are skeletal sentinels below the immense, orange-red sand dunes surrounding the white-clay pan of Sossusvlei. You started at dawn up Dune 45; it's only 550 feet, but the shifting terrain makes it an hour-long trek. Incredibly, the Atlantic Ocean is just 40 miles west of this parched, surreal landscape. Captivated by the otherworldliness, you press on. Nearly 500 miles northeast, Etosha National Park's salt pan seems bone dry, but watering holes here attract zebras, rhinos, elephants, leopards—and small safari camps. Southern Namibia's 100-mile Fish River Canyon is 1,800 feet deep in parts. The river that long ago carved it is now just a series of pools. From a canyon-edge lodge, you drink in the view and an icy Windhoek lager, sating your thirst for Namibia.

Namibia: watering hole in Etosha National Park;
sand dunes in Sossusvlei (right).

The Ends of the Earth

Your long journey south began with a flight to Auckland and a connection to Christchurch. You saw the city—vibrant once more after earthquakes earlier in the decade—and you whale-watched at Kaikoura Peninsula. A helicopter took you to hike above the first icefall at Franz Josef Glacier. Then it was south again to adrenaline-fueled Queenstown, birthplace of bungee jumping, and Te Anau, gateway to Fiordland Park in the South Island's far southwest. The scenery along the drive to Milford Sound was only a teaser. From the 10-mile inlet of the Tasman Sea, mountains like Mitre Peak rise abruptly, verdant with rain forest and punctuated by waterfalls. If this is what the earth's end looks like, you're in no hurry to return to its start.

New Zealand: hiking the Franz Josef Glacier (left); humpback whale in Kaikoura (top right); Milford Sound (bottom right).

Perito Moreno Glacier, Patagonia

Rivers of Ice

The sound is deafening as house-size pieces of ice calve and crash into Lake Argentino's steely waters below the snowcapped Andes. In the Iceberg Channel, the 3-mile Perito Moreno Glacier towers 240 feet above you. It gleams a frosty blue in the late-morning sun. It floats beside your boat. It crunches under your crampons on a guided hike. In coming days, you'll visit El Chaltén, in the northern section of Los Glaciares National Park, to explore trails near the Fitz Roy Range. For now, it's back to El Calafate, where ice cream flavored with the berry for which the city is named makes a fittingly cold finish. Legend holds that one taste of this fruit guarantees your return to Patagonia. It might turn out to be true.

Lost Cities of the Incas

You linger by the campfire under the clear Andean sky. Your guide points out the llama and the serpent, two sacred Inca constellations. You'll soon watch the sun god, Inti, breathe golden color into the stone terraces and ceremonial buildings above you. When explorer Hiram Bingham sought the outpost to which the Incas fled after the Spanish arrived, he began at Choquequirao, the most remote citadel in Peru's Urubamba Valley, the heart of the Inca Empire. To reach it, your group followed 500-year-old footpaths along the raging Apurímac River for two days. Like most visitors, Bingham soon forgot Choquequirao and focused on Machu Picchu. You'll visit it, too. For now, though, you're grateful to have first found the majestic solitude of this other lost city.

Choquequirao ruins, Peru

Here Flows the Lava

Calderas smoke and fume. Lava oozes. Bone-white branches are strewn across patches of brown rock. Such is the landscape created by two massive and very active volcanoes—Kilauea and Mauna Loa—in Hawaii Volcanoes National Park on the Big Island. Take short day hikes along Devastation Trail or to Kilauea's Iki Crater, or drive the 19-mile Chain of Craters Road, which pairs volcanic views with those of the vast Pacific. As darkness descends, the red lava really burns to life. Go on a nighttime hike for an up-close look at its glow. Or book a moonlight sail or helicopter tour. The National Park Service always knows where the action is: Check its daily lava-flow updates.

Volcanoes National Park, Big Island, HI

Surf's Up

You look back: This is your wave. Concentrate: paddle, push up, stand up. You're on your board, gliding toward Waikiki Beach. Modern surfing began on this Honolulu bay, whose slow-rolling waves make it your ideal starting point, too. It's hard to stay focused, though. Tomorrow, you plan to see the North Shore's huge waters, driving up Oahu's center, stopping at pineapple plantations and the surf shops of Haleiwa. Or maybe you'll drive the Windward Side, through the Koolau Mountains, stopping at viewpoints and the Polynesian Cultural Center before reaching Ehukai Beach, where pros ride the 40-foot Banzai Pipeline in winter, and Waimea Bay. Your mind snaps back to Waikiki—and you lose your balance. No matter. There are plenty more waves in the sea.

Oahu, HI: Waimea Bay (top); surfing off the North Shore.

A Desert Star

Look up. On a moonless night, your to-do list in California's Joshua Tree National Park, one of America's best for stargazing, is the sum total of those two words. What will you see? Oh, just the heavenly sprawl of the Milky Way illuminating what seems like the entire northern hemisphere. Skip the motel rooms of nearby towns, and, instead, pitch a tent or park your RV at one of nearly 500 hundred campsites the park provides for this IMAX-like spectacle. Although you'll see photographers setting up cameras on tripods for long-exposure and time-lapse shots, most folks are content to simply huddle around a desert bonfire and let the sky—and the park itself—work its timeless magic.

Joshua Tree National Park, CA

Life After Death

Hottest. Driest. Darkest. Lowest. Flattest. It's hard to process the superlatives associated with Death Valley, a national park and biosphere reserve filling 3 million California and Nevada acres. But understanding seeps in as you gaze out over the folded sandstone hills from Zabriskie Point or walk over the dry, cracked earth of the Racetrack Playa. You sense the powerful draw of the desert, the one that attracted prospectors and entrepreneurs to this vast network of salt flats, lake beds, and cinder cones. Imagine yourself a miner at the Rhyolite Ghost Town, or tour Scotty's Castle, a Roaring Twenties–era hideaway. Poolside at the Inn at Furnace Creek is the place to be on hot afternoons, before a not-to-be-missed stargazing excursion out on the flats.

Death Valley, CA/NV: predawn light over Zabriskie Point (top);
Rhyolite Ghost Town.

Yosemite's Glacier Point

Is there a bad time to experience Glacier Point, one of Yosemite National Park's most glorious overlooks? Let's see. . . . Drive up before sunrise in summer to watch the slow illumination of Yosemite Valley. Check. On a winter's day, snowshoe up Glacier Point Road to see the Sierras draped in several feet of snow. Check. In spring through fall, hike Four Mile Trail and catch the midday California sun lighting the rock formations and waterfalls equally. Check. Hang around for sunset to see the day's final orange-red rays strike Half Dome, and stick around to stargaze and sneak peeks on telescopes set up by amateur astronomers. Check and check. Ah, Glacier Point: Yosemite, perfected.

Yosemite National Park: Glacier Point (left); Yosemite Valley, Merced River, and El Capitan formation

A Redwood Coast

It's hard to know where to look: up at the 300-foot coast redwoods or down at the deep-green sword fern and redwood sorrel undergrowth along the path. You'll probably be compelled to alternate the direction of your gaze in any of California's 40 state and national parks that preserve the *Sequoia sempervirens*. Whether you're strolling in Muir Woods National Monument (just 10 miles from the Golden Gate Bridge) or hiking through fog-shrouded stands in Redwood National Park en route to secluded Enderts Beach, the sight of these 1,000-year-old giants will be burned in your memory forever.

Redwood National Park, CA

A Green Laboratory

The ecological term "biota" refers to the collective animal and plant life of a particular region. Out on the Hoh Rain Forest's moss- and fern-draped paths, the sheer *volume* of biota—especially the flora—makes you feel as if you've landed on an entirely different planet. This corner of Washington State, home to Olympic National Park, gets enough rainfall (over 12 feet a year!) not only to make its Sitka spruces and Western hemlocks tower, but also to make all sorts of impossibly green growth thrive on every surface within the forest. Even if you wear a poncho, prepare to get wet. It's all part of the experience—as is warming up with a hot toddy at day's end in a B&B.

Hoh Rain Forest, Olympic National Park, WA

Sunset in the West

As the sun dips behind Sitka spruce–covered Tskawahyah Island, the tidal pools dotting Cape Alava's shoreline turn fiery red, signaling the westernmost sunset in the Lower 48. What you've just witnessed is well worth the 3-mile boardwalk hike, through a sea of ferns and other impossibly green undergrowth, from Lake Ozette. For that matter, it's worth the 1,200-mile hike along the Pacific Northwest National Scenic Trail from Montana's Chief Mountain border crossing. Either way, you've made it to the lush million-acre Pacific Northwest wonderland of Olympic National Park. Pitch a tent, and let the crash of the waves and the sight of the stars (or, more likely, the region's famous moody fog) lull you to sleep. America bids you good night.

Cape Alava, Olympic National Park, WA

Flying High at Base Camp

You've decided to let it all hang out with some paragliding . . . or maybe not, opting instead for a leisurely (four-wheel!) drive up Trail Creek Road. Either way, you'll be looking *down* on Ketchum—though the town is itself at 6,000 feet amid the Sawtooth National Forest. The same is true of the views from atop 9,000-foot Bald Mountain, which pierces the sky above Idaho's aptly named Sawtooth Range and is home to the 3,400-foot vertical drop of the highly regarded Sun Valley Ski Resort. After a day's worth of soaring, hiking, fishing, rafting, biking, or skiing, you head into the quintessential mountain town itself and share tales of your exploits at Whiskey Jacques' or the Cellar Pub.

Ketchum, ID: Top of the Elephants Perch, Sawtooth Mountains; a view of town and Sun Valley (right).

The Earth Bubbles Up

Bubbling pools, powerful geysers, electric colors, stunning canyons, rampaging wildlife, quiet lakes, and classic lodges—Yellowstone National Park pretty much has it all. Tough to get to and hard to leave, the park has been wowing folks for centuries. The soaring Lincoln Log–style Old Faithful Inn, built in 1904, is a great base from which to explore, and it's just steps from the daily performances of the Old Faithful Geyser and the deep blues and oranges of the Morning Glory Pool. And sights like the cascading levels of the Grand Prismatic Spring and the craggy gorge of the Grand Canyon of the Yellowstone will be forever burned in your memory as some of the most awe-inspiring landscapes you've ever witnessed.

Yellowstone National Park, MT/WY/ID: Yellowstone Canyon (left); Castle Geyser.

Mountain Days, Rodeo Nights

Get one glimpse of the Tetons, and you'll never forget them. Rising more than 7,000 feet above the Jackson Hole Valley floor (itself 6,000 feet above sea level), the range seems almost grafted onto the Wyoming landscape. Days are spent hiking in Grand Teton National Park, boating across Jenny Lake, riding the tram at Jackson Hole Mountain Resort, and spotting bison grazing in the valley. As the sun sets, switch out your hiking gear for some cowboy boots and a 10-gallon hat—you'll blend right in at the family-friendly Jackson Hole Rodeo, held several nights a week between May and September. The perfect rodeo pairing? Some roast rack of lamb or beef tenderloin at the Blue Lion.

Grand Teton National Park, WY

Where the
Buffalo Roam

Park yourself by the fire at the stone-and-timber Sylvan Lake Lodge, listen to the crackle of burning ponderosa pine, and get out one of the Custer State Park brochures. It's time to decide what you'll do tomorrow—will it be some trout fishing at Stockade Lake? A horseback ride to the cabin at Badger Hole? A day hike to Lovers Leap overlooking the Black Hills? Or just a lazy drive along the Needles Highway, with stops to photograph the park's herd of over 1,000 free-range bison? No matter what you choose, you'll be in one of South Dakota's crown jewels, sharing it—and sometimes the roads through it—with elk, bighorn sheep, mule deer, mountain goats, and the ubiquitous prairie dog.

Custer State Park, SD

Geology on Display

As you head east on a deserted stretch of Highway 24 out of Torrey, Utah, a stunning sight rises from the Colorado Plateau: striated sandstone cliffs in colors ranging from almond white to ruddy brown. The Waterpocket Fold—so called for its accordion-like layers of rock—runs for a 100 miles north to south through Capitol Reef National Park. Day hikes take you to formations, petroglyphs, and even a 3,000-tree orchard planted by Mormons in the 1880s. Twilight emboldens the hues here, so why not pitch a tent in the Fruita Campground's lush green grass and watch the sunset play with the palette?

Capitol Reef National Park, UT

Springboard to Adventure

At the end of the day, you'll no doubt be soaking those tired bones in a claw-foot tub at the Sorrel River Ranch Resort & Spa. But right now, it's time to fuel up with some eggs smothered in green chile from the Moab Diner. Don't worry, though—you'll be burning off those calories soon enough. The stunning scenery surrounding this Utah town just begs to be actively explored. Hike under fiery red sandstone formations in Arches and Canyonlands national parks, and raft the deep cuts made by the mighty Colorado River. Bike through tall stands of aspen and maple in Manti-La Sal National Forest, and take in awe-inspiring sunset canyon views from Dead Horse Point.

Around Moab, UT: Arches National Park (left);
Canyonlands National Park.

The Painted Desert

The strata of buttes and mesas in Arizona's Petrified Forest National Park range in color from reds, oranges, yellows, and greens to purples, blues, grays, and whites. To take in this study of contrasts in a day, depart early from the park's northeast corner, home to the elegant, modernist Painted Desert Visitors Center and historic Painted Desert Inn, a onetime Route 66 stop. A 28-mile drive passes eight scenic viewpoints; Puerco Pueblo archaeological site; petroglyph-covered Newspaper Rock; and Jasper Forest, one of several spots where wood has turned to stone. Trails like the Crystal Forest, Agate House, and Giant Logs invite deeper exploration. Time things well, and you'll reach the park's southwest corner, and the Rainbow Forest Museum, before dusk.

Petrified Forest National Park, AZ

Across the Great Divide

Elk graze the high grass. Bighorn sheep jump from rock to rock, surefooted and spry even at an elevation of 10,000 feet. Moose walk amid willows flanking the Colorado River. You snap photos of Milner Pass and wander a treeless, windswept mountaintop for more panoramic shots—from 12,000 feet—of Rocky Mountain National Park. Like the pioneers, you're awestruck by the immense beauty of the Continental Divide. But your journey is far less daunting. A winding but smooth drive takes you down into woodsy Estes Park. You relax in the beer garden at Estes Park Brewery, tuck in to venison at Twin Owls Steakhouse, and soak in your cabin's hot tub beside the Big Thompson River. It's the contemporary end to a classic crossing.

Rocky Mountain National Park, CO

The Gulf Coast, Naturally

Great blue herons elegantly step through windblown sand dunes and seaweed jettisoned all the way from the Sargasso Sea. The breeze picks up a bit as seagulls cruise overhead and sea turtles prowl the shore. Occasionally—but just occasionally—a hissing of the sands indicates the approach of a jeep or SUV driving past your campsite, artfully placed somewhere along the 70-mile undeveloped stretch of Padre Island National Seashore on the Texas Gulf Coast. Some kite-surfing or deep-sea fishing, a beach bonfire, and a fiery red sunset over the 1,300-mile Intracoastal Waterway running parallel to the world's longest barrier island are about all you need down here, miles from the nearest city—or even the nearest road.

Padre Island, TX

Rain Forest in Paradise

Please don't go to Puerto Rico and only sit on the beach. Yes, it's tempting. And yes, the beaches—and the tropical drinks—are perfect. But you'd be missing a fabulous sight: El Yunque National Forest. This tropical rain forest is just 25 miles east of San Juan and a few miles inland from the Wyndham Grand Rio Mar Resort (a perfect base from which to explore). Bring hiking gear, but make sure your bathing suit is underneath. You want to be ready to dive into the pool under La Mina Falls at the end of one of the most popular hikes. Another can't miss: a hike or drive up to the park's stone observation towers, which offer panoramic views of this island paradise.

El Yunque National Forest, PR: La Mina Falls (left);
jungle canopy beneath Los Picachos.

A Parade of Birds

A black-and-white anhinga takes flight after spotting some prey. A great blue heron delicately wades into the saw-grass marsh. A wood stork pokes its long, hooked bill into the mud for worms. An osprey gazes down from a cypress tree. It's an endless pageant in Everglades National Park, an International Biosphere Reserve that is, almost impossibly, a mere hour's drive from Miami's busy South Beach. The Anhinga Trail alone teems with birds, turtles, alligators, crocodiles, and other wildlife, along with a slightly more mundane species: the amateur photographer. To leave humanity well behind, head just a few miles deeper into the park— by canoe to Nine Mile Pond or on foot to Mahogany Hammock.

Everglades National Park, FL

Wild, Wild Horses

It's not a rumor: Herds of horses do roam freely on the sands of Maryland's Assateague State Park and Assateague Island National Seashore. Admire their grace from a distance, as they're truly wild. With a proper, over-the-sand vehicle (and permits), you can drive on the 37-mile-long barrier island, but hiking the dunes is far more intimate. And horses aren't the only wildlife you'll spot—the island is on a migratory flyway used by great egrets and snow geese. Watch for fiddler crabs and sea turtles while beachcombing the swaths of sand. There's no need to rush: Pitch a tent and camp overnight on the beach to the sounds of crashing Atlantic waves and the sight of a star-filled sky.

Assateague Island, MD

The Wind and the Heather

Savor the moment when your ferry docks on Nantucket Island. You've arrived at a very special, pristine Massachusetts sanctuary—of both nature and history. The cobblestone streets of the colonial harbor are lined with cedar-shingled houses; cozy B&Bs; and top-shelf cuisine at restaurants like Dune, Straight Wharf, and Company of the Cauldron. When you leave town, it's to explore the beaches and dunes of this rough, windswept island, either by jeep or bike. A leisurely cycle out east to Sankaty Head Light, built in 1850, is a good bucket-list item, as is a longer ride up to Great Point Light. Your reward? An ice-cold Whale's Tale Pale Ale from Cisco Brewery, before or after a peek at the Whaling Museum.

Nantucket Island, MA: Straight Wharf waterfront (left);
Sankaty Head Light.

Acadia National Park, ME

Sunrise in the East

The alarm goes off at 4:30 am. You stumble around, getting dressed and pouring coffee into a thermos. You drive in darkness to the top of Mount Desert Island's 1,500-foot Cadillac Mountain, the highest point in Acadia National Park. You and a few others amble along a path, reaching the edge of a cliff in time for America's first sunrise. Once the mighty Atlantic is illuminated, it's time for an omelet back at your B&B in picturesque Bar Harbor. And the day continues in earnest. Acadia is a microcosm of Maine's spectacular 3,400-mile coast, and its cliffs, coves, beaches, fishing villages, and ferries to islets await early risers like you.

Index of Places

The West

South & Central America